RADIOHEAD

coming up for air

by Steve Malins

DEDICATION: for Alice

Thanks to: Caffy and Terry at Hall or Nothing, Mark
Paytress at Record Collector and Simon Harper for
their assistance in researching this book.

Picture research
Mark Ranaldi

Design
William Harvey

First published in Great Britain in 1997 by Virgin Publishing

Virgin

332 Ladbroke Grove
London
W10 5AH
© JMP Ltd. All rights reserved.

A catalogue record for this book is available from the British Library
ISBN 0 7535 01252

INTRODUCTION

Thom Yorke's spindly frame was leaning against a chromed fitness machine in an Oxford health club when I met him for the first time in February 1995. The limply inactive, scrawled-up figure seemed all the more frail in these surroundings, as if the torrid sessions for Radiohead's freshly minted album The Bends had literally drawn all the air out of him.

Over the course of the next three hours I found him to be far more candid than his dour reputation had suggested, despite the fact that his head cold turned into full-blown flu after he jumped into the club's swimming pool for the photo session.

That interview for Vox magazine was their first cover feature in the major British music press and I've drawn heavily on it in this book, including material which has never been published before. Although I spent more time with Thom, the gregarious Colin Greenwood, the shy reserve of his younger brother Jonny and the affable chattiness offered by Phil Selway and Ed O'Brien added up to an open discussion of the remarkable changes they'd been through together since they met up at Abingdon Boys School in Oxfordshire back in the mid 70s.

After the hellish promotional schedule which followed the success of the single Creep in the States and "difficult" sessions for their second album The Bends, Radiohead emerged at the start of 1995 as a real force. The Bends was arguably the best album of a very good year, revealing greater emotional depth than Blur, Pulp or Oasis, but it lacked the killer single which would finally shake off their underdog reputation in their home country. Given that the hype for Britpop has faded and threatens to turn against its main protagonists, maybe Radiohead's outsider status will serve them well in 1997 as they prepare to release their third album.

One of the first things he ever bought me was a pair of boxing gloves," remembers the 5' 5" singer. "He used to try to teach me to box, but whenever he hit me I'd fall flat on my ass

Thom Yorke: *"Songwriting for me is therapy. Most creativity comes out of some kind of crisis, and the coolest rock 'n' roll bands are people who can deal with that and admit to their problems."*

Thom Yorke was born in Wellingborough, Northamptonshire on 7 October 1968. His father sold chemical-engineering equipment, a job which took the family north to a remote part of Scotland when Thom was still a toddler. The youngster's introspective personality absorbed the stark scenery around his home which was near a beach covered with World War II bunkers and barbed wire. Yorke's father had been a champion boxer at university and he tried to encourage his skinny, delicate-looking son to have a go. "One of the first things he ever bought me was a pair of boxing gloves," remembers the 5' 5" singer. "He used to try to teach me to box, but whenever he hit me I'd fall flat on my ass."

Yorke's obsession with medical imagery in Radiohead songs is rooted in his childhood. "When I was born my left eye was completely paralysed," he told me, propped up against a fitness machine. "My eyelid was permanently shut and they thought it would be like that for the rest of my life. Then some specialist bloke realised he could graft a muscle in, like a bionic eye. So I had five major operations between the age of nought and six. They fucked up the last one and I went half blind. I can kind of see. I can judge if I'm going to hit something but that's just about it. They made me go around with a patch on my eye for a year, saying, 'Oh well, it's just got lazy through all the operations,' which was crap because they'd just damaged it. The first operation I had, I was just learning to speak, and apparently I said, 'What have I got?' I didn't know. I woke up and I had this huge thing on my eye, and according to my parents, I just doubled up and started crying.

"Hospitals are fucking horrifying places. We were next to the geriatric ward as well so we used to get these senile old men coming in, walking into things and throwing up. There was no television, no phones, just the radio."

The singer's problems got worse when he was seven and his family moved to Oxford, where he attended the Standlake Church of England School. This self-confessed "strange child" was older and more self-conscious, and now had to face new classmates. "The only thing that affected me really badly was walking around with a patch on my eye for a year, with everybody taking the piss out of me. I was starting to become more self-conscious and that was about the worst thing that anybody could possibly have done, especially as my family moved twice in six months. It meant that I had to face a new classroom, where, unlike my old school friends, they weren't used to the problems I was having with my eye."

When he started at his second school in a few months, Abingdon Boys School, a private school, his new 'mates' gave him the nickname "Salamander". "I didn't like it. I got into a fight with the guy who originated the name but that didn't stop it. It was a very malicious school and everyone had very malicious nicknames, so Salamander was par for the course."

An off-beat incident in his adolescence helped him deal with his self-consciousness. "When I was eighteen I worked in a bar and this madwoman came in and said, 'You have beautiful eyes, but they're completely wrong,'" he explains. "Whenever I get paranoid, I just think about what she said."

Yorke's interest in music was initially fuelled by long hours listening to the radio – his only form of escape. When he was eight his mother encouraged his growing enthusiasm for music by giving him a small Spanish guitar. He set out to be

When I born my was paralysed

My eyelid was permanently shut and they thought it would be like that for the rest of my life. Then some specialist bloke realised he could graft a muscle in, like a bionic eye

was left eye completely

So I had five major operations between the age of nought and six. They fucked up the last one and I went half blind. I can kind of see. I can judge if I'm going to hit something but that's just about it

the next Brian May but he was a slow learner and after a few months all he could play was Kumbaya. He formed his first band at the age of ten, playing a home-made guitar while a friend created bizarre electronic noises by dismantling old TV sets. Their mates would stand around and watch as the spindly youngster strummed some basic chords and his sidekick routed around the television wires, suffering the odd electric shock.

Meanwhile, two Oxford-born brothers were also getting into music at an early age. Born on 26 June 1969, Colin Greenwood was introduced to late 70s new wave acts Joy Division, Magazine and John Cooper Clarke by his older sister. So too was his younger brother Jonathan, who was born on 5 November 1971, although he didn't realise he'd been exposed to this musical influence until years later.

"It's very weird because I didn't listen to any bands really when I was learning to play guitar. I only had one album until I was sixteen, it was Talking Heads I think, and that was all. Quite tragic really. As a result I wasn't interested in guitar players as names. But a couple of years ago our sound man said, "Have you heard of Magazine?" and I said, "I think my older sister used to play me Magazine." So he lent me a CD and of course, not only did I remember every note, but all the words and everything. And this was from when I was seven or eight. It was quite scary how I'd been ripping off and copying John McGeogh [Magazine's guitarist] even though I hadn't started playing guitar until I was fourteen. So basically, thanks a lot. Thank God my sister wasn't playing me AC/DC."

When Jonny was six he bought Squeeze's Cool For Cats on pink vinyl and he would sing songs to the dinner ladies. He spent his childhood in various orchestras, including the Thames Vale Youth Orchestra, playing everything from the recorder to jazz guitar, piano and viola. The brothers' father died when they were young but Colin says his background was like the Von Trapp family, led by his mother who was tone deaf. There was always music in the house, whether it was little Jonny on recorder or Colin cranking up his Joy Division records.

The brothers rarely got into fights with each other. Theirs is a relationship which has maintained an affable sense of friendship, even in the claustrophobia of being in a band together. Colin: "Unlike the Gallaghers we beat each other up in private and get on very well in public... It's really nice to be in a position where you're with a member of your family and you get on really well." However, Colin – who maintains a bizarre politeness towards his brother, whom he always calls Jonathan rather than Jonny – did occasionally change the paints around in their paint boxes. Jonny didn't notice because he's completely colour blind so it's hardly surprising he created a number of "disturbing pictures".

Guitarist Ed O'Brien has been more guarded about his upbringing. He was born in Oxford on 15 April 1968 into a middle-class, "medical family", including his father who is a doctor. Drummer Phil Selway, despite his 'Mad Dog' nickname (so called because of the occasional tantrum which ruptures his usual calm, sensible manner) was born into another middle-class, academically inclined household in Hemingford Grey on 23 May 1967. Both boys attended the same private school in Abingdon as the Greenwoods and Thom Yorke.

The lives of all five band members were strongly influenced by a headmaster whom Thom in particular regarded as a "power-crazed lunatic", focusing most of his "teenage hatred" on this man. "I really grew up with a hatred for him," recalls Thom, "because I thought he was an evil, petty little man with ridiculous sideburns, who used to flick his hair across his head to hide the bald patch. One of those guys. He banned all electric music from the school because there was a punk school band that did a gig that got a bit out of hand, so he banned all pop music.

"Just after I left the head got the idea of becoming a bishop, so he started walking around in bishops' clothing," remembers Thom, smirking, who later wrote a song called Bishop's Robes. "He started preaching in the school assembly, even though he wasn't ordained or anything. And he started forcing people to go to chapel. I still hate him and if I see or hear of him I get this deep sinking feeling."

The headmaster also made a strong impression on Jonny. "He was terrifying. On my last day he dressed up for this church service as a bishop, in the full garb, and he wasn't. It was very bizarre. Personally I think he had a bit of a God complex going on. For me, it just created this horrible atmosphere there but it also gave us all a determination to do something different."

When he was twelve Thom Yorke joined the school punk band TNT and sang as frontman for the first time. No one else wanted to do it so he gave it a go: "I

Unlike the Gallaghers we beat each other up in private
Phil Selway

and get on very well in public... It's really nice to be
Jonny Greenwood

in a position where you're

Ed O'Brien

with a member of your family
and you get on really well

Colin Greenwood

started singing into this little stereo mike tied to the end of a broomstick handle. Everyone just started falling about laughing and that was that. That was my introduction to singing."

Frustrated by big egos in the band, he formed his own group at school with Ed O'Brien "because I thought he was cool and looked like Morrissey; and with Colin (who was also in TNT) because he was in my year and we always ended up at the same parties. He'd be wearing a beret and a catsuit, or something pretty fucking weird and I'd be in a frilly blouse and crushed-velvet dinner suit, and we'd pass around the Joy Division records. I sympathised with him for being in TNT after I left, so I told him he could join if he played bass like Peter Hook. He never did."

Colin Greenwood met O'Brien during a school production of Gilbert & Sullivan's Trial By Jury, but it was Yorke who brought Colin, Ed and Phil together. Selway was in his last year at school when he joined the fledgling band. Once again Yorke took the initiative. The first thing he said to the drummer was, "Can't you play any fucking faster?"

Calling themselves On A Friday because that was the day they all met up and rehearsed, their early gigs were done on the sly. Yorke kept his disapproving parents in the dark whenever the band played live by telling them that he was staying at a friend's house. Still only thirteen, Jonny Greenwood hassled the band for a year to let him join. Finally, Colin asked him to bring along a harmonica. "It was a way of keeping an eye on him," remembers the older brother. "He was only thirteen, it was a difficult age."

Jonny: "I was two or three years younger, snot pouring out of my nose, but I kept bugging them: 'Can I be in your band?'"

A week after the younger brother's first rehearsal, he sat with his harmonica at the side of the stage while On A Friday played at their local venue, the Jericho Tavern. Eventually the thin-boned frontman signalled for him to get up on stage, a nod which officially invited him into the band. Jonny continued to notch up new instruments to play, buying a keyboard as On A Friday became a "cheesy Talking Heads sixth-form band". The line-up expanded further when they decided to bring in two sisters who played saxophone to form a sassy horn section. Any hecklers in the audience were immediately given the middle finger by the sisters.

Colin and Jonny, who were also nicknamed "the sisters" because they were so in tune with their feminine side, shared Thom's lack of parental support. To this day their mother asks them when "all this hideous nonsense is going to stop". Colin: "Jonathan often teases her about all the drug benders he goes on and she sits there saying, 'Oh yes? How nice, dear.' It was funny when we first got signed. She wouldn't tell our grandfather what we were doing because she thought it would finish him off.

"Actually, she's not happy unless she's worrying. Very Radiohead, that."

Academic ambitions for their son also meant that Phil Selway's parents were equally unimpressed by his involvement in a pop band, which he also accepts is "the ultimate indulgence". Only Ed O'Brien received any encouragement. His father is a big music fan who still enjoys picking Ed's brains about the latest releases. According to Selway, "Ed will come home from a rehearsal or touring or whatever, just wanting to relax with a traditional double vodka, and his dad will come in waving the music papers, wanting to discuss the new Primal Scream single."

Outside of the band, Thom Yorke remained a bit of a loner. "The only gang I was ever in kicked me out! I had Velcro buckles on my trainers instead of laces. They thought I was letting their cool down. Bastards." However, after going "through a bad period at school between thirteen and fifteen" he decided he wanted to go to college. "I got my shit together and won two prizes in one year," recalls the singer. "I got an art prize and a music prize, which is funny because I couldn't read music and I couldn't really paint. It was great though – it was the first time I'd ever had any encouragement. I was really, really chuffed, even though I'd only won a £20 book token. No cup or nothing, though I am still on a roll of honour somewhere, I suppose."

For all five band members the effect of being schooled at an all-boys private establishment was to turn the opposite sex into objects of worship and adolescent fear. "Girls didn't figure in our lives for a long time," confesses Yorke. "They were freaks of nature you saw every now and again and wondered how they worked. I think I still feel like that.

"I feel tremendous guilt for any sexual feelings I have, so I end up spending my entire

life feeling sorry for fancying somebody. Even in school I thought girls were so wonderful that I was scared to death of them. I masturbate a lot. That's how I deal with it."

Encounters with the opposite sex often ended up causing ructions with school and parents. "When I was about fifteen, me and my friends invited these girls round," says Yorke. "We were in the bogs – smoking, drinking and generally having a good time – when this right c*** of a teacher caught us. He made us phone our parents and say exactly what we'd done, and said we were going to be expelled. It wasn't a big deal but it completely destroyed my parents. They thought I was going to be a drug-taking lunatic from hell, and that was the end of me. We never even got suspended in the end – the guy was just winding us up. Arsehole."

The singer remembers innocent kisses as a child with greater fondness than the first time he had sex: "Losing my virginity was a lot less spectacular than having my first French kiss," he declares. "I was seven, she was my first girlfriend. We were in the playground and we promised to get married straight afterwards. But then I moved away from Scotland, where I lived, and never saw her again. I was hoping she'd come to our gig there the other night, but she didn't. She probably doesn't remember me at all, but I remember her. Her name was Katie Garson and her dad had a great Lotus car. But losing my virginity was very disappointing. There was lots of mess and horribleness."

These experiences have left their mark. Yorke admits to a sense of insecurity and resentment towards "beauty, and when I say beauty, I'm not referring to men. Women, that's what I mean. Confronted by a beautiful woman I will leave as soon as possible, or hide in a corner until they leave. It's not just that I find them intimidating. It's the hideous way people flock around them. The way people act in front of them. The way they're allowed to believe they're being so fucking clever. Beauty is all about unearnt privilege and power. I am entirely cynical about it.

"I've never met a single beautiful woman I've actually liked. You never actually get close enough to them to work out what the fuck they're about. I think a part of me used to want to know that, but I've lost all will to do so now.

"It's not just beautiful women. I totally fear all women. Ever since I've been at school. I would go for five months without talking to a girl my own age. I don't think it's misogyny. It's the total opposite. It's blatant fear."

I started singing into this little stereo mike tied to the end of a broomstick handle. Everyone just started falling about laughing and that was that. That was my introduction to singing

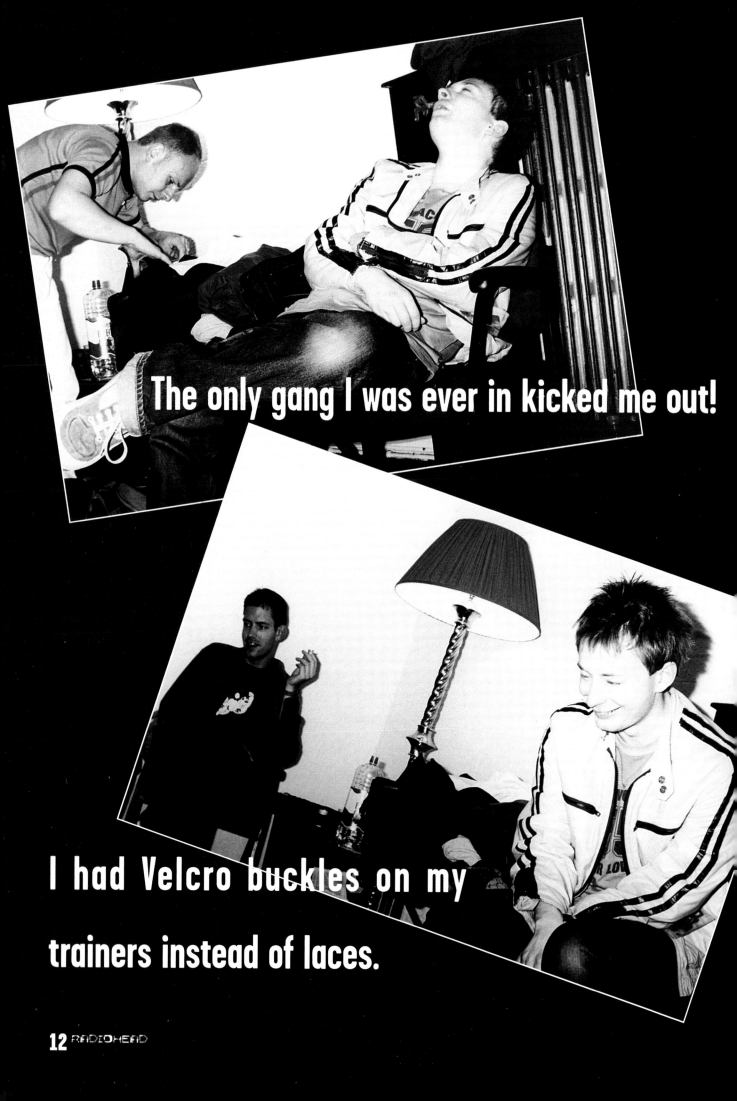

The only gang I was ever in kicked me out!

I had Velcro buckles on my trainers instead of laces.

They thought I was letting their cool down

Bastards

Girls didn't figure in our lives for a long time

They were freaks
of nature you saw
every now and again
and wondered how
they worked

I think I still feel like that

Phil Selway: *"The best thing about Jonny is that he's extremely funny. Naturally funny. He's excellent entertainment value. He usually costs less than a video. The only problem is you can't take him back to the shop when you're sick of him. The worst thing about him is that, especially in stressful situations, he's terribly impatient. He likes everything to be done quickly."*

In 1987 Yorke took a year out after finishing his A-levels and before going to college. He took a part-time job as a sales assistant and his new boss replaced his old headmaster as a new villain in his life: "I used to sell suits for him. This guy was the floor manager of our department, which was menswear. I couldn't afford any of the suits that I was meant to be selling so I used to turn up in an Oxfam suit – which was quite smart – but I still had long blond hair and he took an instant dislike to me. He used to say, 'Why aren't you selling any of your suits?' and I'd say, 'Because they're crap and nobody wants to buy them,' which didn't go down well. He's one of those blokes who'd drive into work, kill a cyclist and not stop.

"One day he took me into his office and accused me of stealing the suits, so I handed my notice in, which was quite a good moment, but I wish I'd told his boss to fuck off because he was even worse – pure scum. He had this twisted little mouth and you could tell he was desperate to make everyone's life hell because his was. Prick."

Yorke was also going through a "tortured", doomed romance at this time. "Have you ever seen Who's Afraid Of Virginia Wolf?" he asked the NME. "It was like that for a year and a half; lots of fighting in public."

From 1987 to 1991 the band were scattered all over the country. Jonny was still at school, while the other three were at different colleges – Selway studied English and History at Liverpool Polytechnic, played drums in a college revue version of Return To The Forbidden Planet and went on to do a post-grad course; Ed O'Brien was up in Manchester University and Colin Greenwood enrolled into Cambridge University where his English Literature degree included a thesis on Raymond Carver. He also became Peterhouse's entertainment officer, blagging occasional gigs for the band in Cambridge.

According to Colin, Peterhouse is "a college known for its reaction against liberal conformism and it's known for being bloody-minded. But I didn't actually apply to Cambridge at first because I didn't think I'd get in, so the first time I saw Peterhouse was when I went up for the interview and it was the last year when there were all men in each year so it was fairly intimidating.

"The thing about Cambridge is there's a lot of pressure on you to be known for something, whether it be journalism, theatre, music or academic studies. It requires a certain amount of confidence to deal with a place like that and if you haven't got it then it can be a bit nightmarish. But any university's the same really. I mean I've played at most of the universities in this country and the kids are the kids, as you say."

Colin and Jonny are considered "frighteningly intelligent" by the other members of the band. "The Greenwoods have a highly intellectual streak to them," reveals Selway. "Colin is the hard-bitten intellect. Jonny is slightly more eccentric." These cerebral characters still dream of pursuing academic studies again in the future. "I entertain this fantasy of going back to college," says Colin, who often suffers from insomnia because of an over-active mind. "I could be this sad Sterling Morrison figure clutching on-to some kind of academic respectability after the ephemeral respectability of pop music."

Jonny echoes his brother when he confesses,

"I entertain this fantasy of going back to college," says Colin, who often suffers from insomnia because of an over-active mind. "I could be this sad Sterling Morrison figure clutching on to some kind of academic respectability after the ephemeral respectability of pop music"

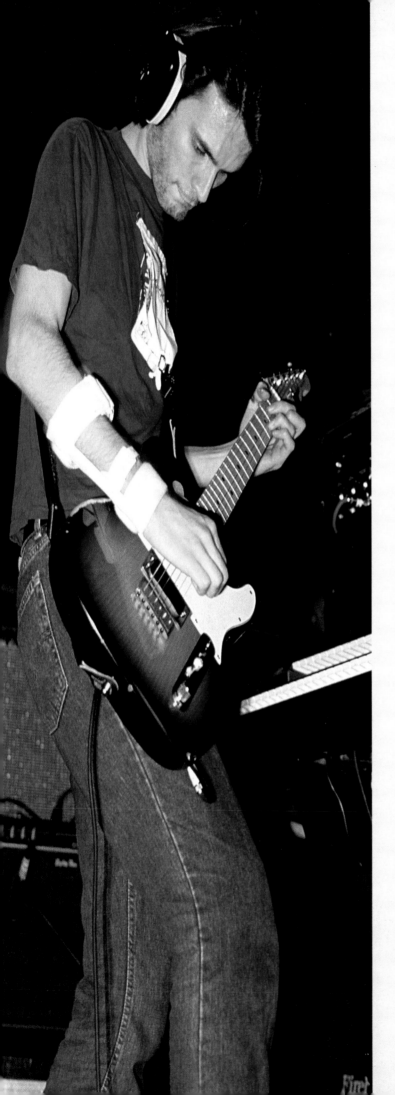

"I have thought about studying later. I've talked to my tutor about doing a course while touring but I'm too lazy for that. Maybe one day."

Meanwhile, in 1988 Yorke began studying English and fine art at Exeter University/College Of Art & Design. He shaved his head, started DJ-ing and experienced the mix of stress and freedom brought by this new independence. "In the first year they said: 'You can do whatever you want.' So I spent a year wandering around saying, 'I don't want to do any of this, actually.' Then by the second year I'd got into computers. I just needed something to start me off and I was all right after that because I'd found a medium in which to work."

One particular area of art interested him which would be reflected in the misfit appeal of Radiohead a few years later: "When I was at college the only artwork I ever really loved was something with this dodgy broad term of 'Outsider Art', which was basically by completely untrained people who'd never been to art college or who were mentally unstable. One of my favourite artists was this, uh, paedophiliac bloke and he did these scribbles which most people would say were like the doodles you do on the telephone.

"But there was something underneath it... There was something about the way he could pick up a pen and put it on a piece of paper, which sounds really wanky but I'd much rather study stuff like that than all the endless fucking Saatchi & Saatchi art, y'know, here's the New Artist For The 90s and aren't they wonderful? I'd much rather go off and explore stuff that didn't come out of that context at all, because that context is self-reverential and boring. I think the same thing is true of the music industry at a lot of points.

"My main problem with the whole Outsider Art thing was one side it could look like a stance, like 'I'm setting myself up,' and I don't want to do that either. Also there's a really nasty element to the Outsider Art thing in the sense that it was a freak show; there were a lot of people who were murderers or emotionally unstable. It wasn't normal housewives; most of them were pretty fucked up one way or another. And so you found that if you read articles it would be about the personalities and not the work."

Yorke was obviously thinking about the personality cults of these artists when he tried to shrug off Radiohead's 90s 'outsider' stance: "I'm very reluctant to agree that we thrive on being outsiders, because that smacks of being a freak show, which I don't think it is."

However, one of On A Friday's earliest songs, Nothing Touches Me, was "based on an artist who was imprisoned for abusing children and spent the rest of his life in a cell painting," reveals Yorke. "But the song is about isolating yourself so much that one day you realise you haven't got any friends any more and no one talks to you."

In addition to hooking up with his old friends for the odd gig at small venues such as London's Rock Garden, Yorke also played lead guitar in a techno band called Flickernoise. The student alcoholic binges hinted at a self-destructive nature. "I almost died from alcohol poisoning once," he confesses. "I lost it for a bit." This boozing was tempered slightly when he met his long-term girlfriend, Rachel. "I've been going out with her since we were at college," he revealed in 1995. "What makes her so desirable? It varies, but at the moment it's the way she looks at people when she's talking to them."

Yorke's tetchy, moody personality meant that it was hardly love at first sight, at least on Rachel's part. "I pursued her, but in all the wrong ways, because I was...terrified of her. You're always terrified of the ones you fancy, yeah? But in my funny way I was very tenacious. It worked out but she did think I was a freak. She really thought I was a freak," he owns up with a smile. "She thought I was impossible to talk to, really moody, difficult, unpleasant and idiotic. And I think I was. But she bashed a lot of that crap out of me."

This self-confessed "flaky twat" craves affection, despite his prickly exterior: "Part of me is always looking for someone to turn around, buy me a drink, give me a hug and say it's all right."

Nevertheless, Rachel's influence hasn't squeezed all the tantrums out of him. "I'm always losing my temper and it's very rarely justified," he allows. "I always feel myself doing it but I can't stop it. Everyone else knows too and no one comes near me. My friends now have the ability to carry on a normal conversation while I blow my top. I should go into therapy, shouldn't I?"

"I almost died from alcohol poisoning once"

"I lost it

for a bit"

"She thought I was impossible to talk to, really moody, difficult, unpleasant and idiotic. And I think I was. But she bashed a lot of that crap out of me."

"I'm always losing my temper and it's very rarely justified," he allows. "I always feel myself doing it but I can't stop it. Everyone else knows too and no one comes near me. My friends now have the ability to carry on a normal conversation while I blow my top. I should go into therapy, shouldn't I?"

CHAPTER THREE
Prove yourself

Jonny on Thom: *"Thom's very quiet. He gets tense very quickly. He's moody and childish and often aloof, but he can also be very affectionate and friendly. He's childish because in the space of 20 minutes he can go through a dozen different moods. He always ends up being portrayed as this miserable complainer. He can be like that, but you should see him in the studio. See how excited and childlike he can be. He's a very volatile person to be around. Sometimes I'm just practising guitar and he'll start feeding me all these incredible ideas. It's like being around Elvis Costello. It's quite alarming really."*

At the turn of the decade, three of the band, Ed O'Brien, Phil Selway and Colin Greenwood, returned to Oxford after completing their studies in the summer.

O'Brien worked as a barman and photographer's assistant, while Phil 'Mad Dog' Selway settled into a job as a desk editor and also did a bit of English language teaching. Cambridge graduate, Colin, exasperated his mother by working for the next nine months in an Our Price shop, in order to "broaden his musical knowledge". He continues, "My mother couldn't believe that I'd got into Cambridge because originally my school said I wasn't intellectually able to do A-levels. So she couldn't believe I spent nine months after I graduated working at Our Price in Oxford. Even the fucking bank manager at NatWest gave me a lecture about having a degree from Cambridge and selling records, and I stupidly said, 'Well I'm going to be in a band' and he was like, 'Come on, get real and wise up, boy.' So when our first record came out it was a nice 'fuck you' to all those people, though not to my mother obviously. She was more upset about my younger brother Jonny joining the band because he dropped out of Oxford."

Jonny left his psychology and music course after

"My mother couldn't believe that I'd got into Cambridge because originally my school said I wasn't intellectually able to do A-levels... even the fucking bank manager at NatWest gave me a lecture about having a degree from Cambridge and selling records, and I stupidly said, 'Well I'm going to be in a band' and he was like, 'Come on, get real and wise up, boy.'

only three months (he's the only member of Radiohead who doesn't have a degree), enabling the band to re-group in Oxford and resolve to take their musical ambitions more seriously. When Thom Yorke left college in summer '91, he started writing songs with Jonny, who had made rapid progress on the guitar despite only taking it up in his mid-teens.

The pair spent hours listening to The Pixies and Lou Reed's New York album, shaping a new, tougher style. The sax-playing sisters were finally ditched, along with their favourite encore, Elvis Costello's anti-hype single, Pump It Up. Some of the new songs were recorded on a four-track demo which was subsequently wiped clean by Colin when he tried to add some "shouty" backing vocals. Several tracks were written about Oxford, including Jerusalem and Everybody Lies Through Their Teeth. "It's such a weird place," explained Thom in the band's first ever inter-view in Curfew magazine, "and it's very important to my writing."

The band also went out busking together and on one occasion local heroes Ride, who were at the height of their fame in the early 90s, stopped to listen to some of their new songs. Usually, however, they reverted to REM covers, which proved to be the only way to make a bit of cash.

The first gig of this reformed band was at the Hollybush Inn, Oxford, on July 22 1991, faced by a "good-sized" crowd and one EMI A&R man. Although Jonny contributed a bit of organ to their set, the inclusion of three guitarists in the line-up gave their sound a new edge and speeded up their songwriting, as the three players, Thom, Jonny and Ed, competed with each other. "Having three guitarists, there's a lot of competition," says Yorke, "about who's going to come up with the best line first. Jonny always wins."

Two weeks later they played at the

"Having three guitarists, there's a lot of competition," says Yorke, "about who's going to come up with the best line first. Jonny always wins."

Tavern and not only was the venue filled to capacity but there were also 25 A&R men there and they all paid to get in. Over the next three months an A&R frenzy over the band showed they were right to take their ambitions more seriously. They recorded their most professional demos to date when they went into Courtyard Studios with Chris Hufford, who had recently produced 'shoegazing' band, Slowdive. "He heard about us through a mutual friend and came to see us at the Jericho," remembers Colin Greenwood. "Afterwards he was almost shaking. He said we were the best group he'd seen in three years and invited us to record with him at the Courtyard. We see it as an investment." Five songs were completed in these sessions, described by Oxford's Curfew magazine as "a massive leap from their last demo, impressive though it was".

Hufford and his business partner at Courtyard Studios in Abingdon, Bryce Edge, also agreed to manage the group, a commitment which has remained despite their later involvement in another Oxford band, Supergrass. Thom told the Curfew journalist, "People sometimes say we take things too seriously but it's the only way you'll get anywhere. We're not going to sit around and wait and just be happy if something turns up. We are ambitious. You have to be."

Shortly after this interview in summer '91, they signed to Parlophone Records, still calling themselves On A Friday. Yorke set out the band's determination to avoid the dead-end cliques of the indie scene: "We never wanted to be the most exciting band in our ghetto. The idea was to cut straight through all that 'paying your dues' shit and get the whole world to see us. That was part of the attraction that our record deal offered us. The contract signed us to Parlophone 'all around the world and in the known and unknown universe.' I like that breadth of vision."

"People sometimes say we take things too seriously but it's the only way you'll get anywhere."

"We're not going to sit around and wait and just be happy if something turns up. We are ambitious. You

By the start of '92 they'd changed their name to Radiohead, the title of a song on Talking Heads' True Stories album. They started gigging furiously on the indie circuit through the year, supporting everyone from Sultans Of Ping to James, Kingmaker and Dr & The Medics. They released their first EP in May 1992, led by the track Prove Yourself which was built around the typically self-deprecating line, "I'm better off dead." It was a raw, impressive debut, with Prove Yourself becoming their first ever song played on the radio when Radio One DJ Gary Davies nominated it as "Happening Track Of The Week".

Their follow-up, Creep, released in September, was even more impressive. Yorke had written this self-loathing anthem while still at college but the song burst into life when Jonny Greenwood tried to sabotage the inferiority complex expressed by the words with a hacking, snarly guitar noise just before the chorus. Yorke: "That nervous twitch he [Jonny] does, that's just his way of checking that the guitar is working, that it's loud enough, and he ended up doing it while we were recording. And while we were listening to it, it was like 'Hey, what the fuck was that? Keep that! Do that!'" Yorke was equally effacing about the song's lines: "I wasn't very happy with the lyrics. I thought they were pretty crap." Other tracks on the EP, notably Inside My Head, hinted at the "strangeness" they all felt after ditching academia for a record contract. For the moment both critics and the public cold-shouldered the band and Creep was swiftly deleted after selling only 6,000 copies.

Released in February '93, their next single, Anyone Can Play Guitar, mixed gutsy, anthemic rock with a tune reminiscent of 60s band The Hollies. It reached 32 in the UK charts. The lyrics took a swipe at the arrogance and posturing of rock stars. Yorke's fridge full of unopened beers in 1993, which were left over from the riders at recent gigs with PJ Harvey,

Moonshake and Gallon Drunk, backed up their foppish hatred of what the singer called "hair bands". Throughout his life Yorke has focused his hatred on something - hospitals, his old headmaster, his old boss. Now he directed his venom towards rival bands and the media who were often indifferent to Radiohead and certainly suspicious of their middle-class, university-educated background.

The following month their muted, hurriedly recorded debut album, Pablo Honey, peaked at 25 in the British charts before hurrying out of the Top 75. Most of it was produced and engineered by the American duo Sean Slade and Paul Kolderie, although some earlier tracks recorded with Chris Hufford also found their way on to the final tracklisting. This was part of the problem as there was an unevenness in sound, style and quality. The glue that held Pablo Honey together was the visceral power of Yorke's voice, which crooned and snarled through self-hating, splenetic lyrics. "Pablo Honey is really extreme because I was deliberately projecting all these things personally on to me," says Yorke, "but only to give it extra meaning. It could be completely calculated but it was just personal bits of me and I thought the best place to put it was in a song."

Although he expressed some extreme emotions on Pablo Honey, he soon began to express reservations about their debut. "I liked the first album but we were very naive. We didn't really know how to use the studio." Although there were some brilliant highlights – notably the three singles, along with Thinking About You, Vegetable and Stop Whispering – these doubts were echoed by the critics, many of whom dismissed Radiohead as a home counties grunge band. However, others showed a little more insight, with one journalist accurately summing up the debut as "a patchwork quilt of incandescent brilliance and dulled, formulaic AOR. Pablo Honey was lashed together with more thought to speed and practicality than vision and endurance."

Thom Yorke: *"When I was much younger, I did this four-track demo and this girl, a really close friend of mine, listened to it and said 'Your lyrics are crap. They're too honest, too personal, too direct and there's nothing left to the imagination,' and I've had that in the back of my mind ever since."*

Bizarrely, the first place Creep turned Radiohead into stars was Israel, where the band were mobbed on their first visit to the country. However, bigger things were hinted at when San Francisco's KITS (Live 105) station started playing an import version of Creep in spring '93. The Los Angeles station K-ROQ soon took up the baton and by the summer Creep was their second most requested song. It was then released in the States, spent several months crawling up the Billboard 100, and finally reached its highest placing of number 34 on 4 September thanks to radio support and heavy rotation of the video on MTV. The song described by Rolling Stone as "the most audacious pop move since the Police's Every Breath You Take" fixed Thom Yorke in the mind of the American

The fame of Creep created Ed O'Brien recalls how and say, 'Hey, are you the he's about to react and wave our arms around and 'Creep' guys.'"

its own strange notoriety. "people come up to Thom 'Creep' guy?' You can see that's where we all leap in, go, 'Yeah man, we're the

"Everyone sets me up to be Mr Serious Of Rock which is ridiculous. I used to take myself very seriously, so I suppose I asked for it. Oh well, it could be worse, I could be a Mod, for example."

public as "that Creep guy".

The fame of Creep created its own strange notoriety. Ed O'Brien recalls how "people come up to Thom and say, 'Hey, are you the 'Creep' guy?' You can see he's about to react and that's where we all leap in, wave our arms around and go, 'Yeah man, we're the 'Creep' guys.'"

Yorke had created a monster. "The one thing I regret about that song is people identifying me as the creep," he complained. "Everyone sets me up to be Mr Serious Of Rock which is ridiculous. I used to take myself very seriously, so I suppose I asked for it. Oh well, it could be worse, I could be a Mod, for example." The song's self-hatred became twisted in the minds of some fans. Yorke explained that the scariest interpretation of Creep "would have to be the time I got a letter from a convicted murderer. Basically he said he identified with me. How did it feel? Fuck! Like someone walked over your fucking grave.

"He said, 'I'm the creep in that song. I killed this bloke. They made me do it. It wasn't me, it was the words in my head.'"

The success of Creep effectively dominated Radiohead's schedules through most of 1993, setting themselves up in situations which infuriated Yorke in particular and left the others squirming with embarrassment. Feeling indebted to K-ROQ for the station's support, the singer

"I love getting stoned, it's the best thing in the fuck-ing world. We put together a lot of this album when we were stoned. Shit, I've said it now."

"This absolutely beautiful girl comes up and says, 'My parents are away, do you want to come back with me and do loads of coke?' I didn't have a girlfriend at the time and we had a day off the next day but I was just flabbergasted. I was very polite but I thought of us as a very moral band and I said 'no' because I wasn't sure what the others would think of me."

found himself emotionally blackmailed into recording an acoustic version of Creep for a jingle which declared the show was "so fucking special". The band also appeared on K-ROQ's Love Lines, a phone-in show where people ring in for advice about their problems. "We were assured that it was very amusing and all we had to do was to be humorous," says Jonny, "and the first question is, 'I'm being abused by my father, my boyfriend's beating me up, I'm taking heroin and it's affecting my sex life, what should I do?' I certainly couldn't give an amusing soundbite followed by some hard, up-tempo rock 'n' roll to the LA audience. We do get letters like that as well and obviously you write back. I suppose the nature of the band does attract a lot of those kind of responses and people. We do meet a lot of people who aren't very articulate or whatever."

Radiohead also played Creep at the MTV Beach Party where they performed next to a swimming pool surrounded by the kind of Baywatch-perfect bodies which Yorke has so openly resented. "Schedules. That was my whole life," he says. "Things were being thrown at us all the time, like, 'You're doing the Arsenio Hall show tomorrow' and no one tells you why. But it all went sour because we couldn't... get rid of the song. We had to milk it. And the album was never given a chance."

On the back of the single, Pablo Honey did

"I've never taken advantage of the opportunity of one-night stands"

"It's like treating sex like sneezing. Sex is a fairly disgusting sort of tufted, smelly-area kind of activity, which is too intimate to engage in with strangers. I'm all for the erotic in terms of imagination, but the physical side is something different."

reach the American Top 40 with sales of nearly a million, but it didn't bury into the national psyche as deeply as Creep. Worryingly, a lot of people knew the song but couldn't remember the name of the band and certainly had no idea what the accompanying album was called.

Meanwhile, the promotion continued unabated. The hype reached a ludicrous level when they arrived at the LA base of their American label, Capitol Records, to discover that everyone in the building had been given a Radiohead T-shirt to wear that day. To make matters worse, the band's attempts to send up their success in the States backfired on them. They began to present themselves as tea-drinking English fops, "low on testosterone" but enthusiastic about playing bridge. This only served to emphasise their college-boy pasts and suggested further comparisons between Radiohead and The Fixx, a pompous, middle-class act in the 80s who were big in the States but were never taken seriously in their own country.

In 1995 Yorke wound up for

Noodle adverts than there is in Animal Nitrate or anything by Bikin

song I've heard this year. There's more art in the Tango and Pot

r Cornershop."

another attack, half exasperated at the band's own folly, as he snapped, "Well, all that tea-drinking stuff is complete bollocks obviously. We were trying to keep it as a joke, but the joke wore thin because it didn't have any basis in reality at all after a while. The reality is that we were probably doing as much drugs as everybody else. I wouldn't go on a chat show and talk about it, because its purely recreational. I love getting stoned, it's the best thing in the fucking world. We put together a lot of this album when we were stoned. Shit, I've said it now." He sounded uncomfortable and unconvincing as he continued, "I go through phases of drinking myself into the ground. I'm just one of those people who binges. I did last week in Los Angeles, I was drinking all the time." Perhaps embarrassed by this half-hearted attempt at rock 'n' roll swagger, he sank his teeth into the old image again. "We're not tea-drinking, card-playing idiots. In fact, the others have tried to play bridge recently but no one could get it together, so that period has definitely passed us by."

The band's dubious rock 'n' roll credentials were further undermined after Ed O'Brien owned up to a "holier than thou attitude" when on tour, especially "after a gig in Dallas" two years ago in 1993. "This absolutely beautiful girl comes up and says, 'My parents are away, do you want to come back with me and do loads of coke?' I didn't have a girlfriend at the time and we had a day off the next day but I was just flabbergasted. I was very polite but I thought of us as a very moral band and I said 'no' because I wasn't sure what the others would think of me."

This gentlemanly reaction is typical of all the band members. "I tend to run away if it's anything beyond them saying they like the music," says Thom of female fans. "We were at a single sex school so... you know... Anyway I have someone that I love. So it's... nice."

Jonny was also affected by his lack of experience with girls in his teens: "I've never taken advantage of the opportunity of one night stands. It's like treating sex like sneezing. Sex is a fairly disgusting sort of tufted, smelly-area kind of activity, which is too intimate to engage in with strangers. I'm all for the erotic in terms of imagination, but the physical side is something different."

Back in the UK, Radiohead released the "universally panned" Pop Is Dead single in May, which stalled outside the Top 40. Yorke explained

"I'm still upset that no one

seems to care about us in Britain,"

the barbed sentiments of the song as a reaction to the things "what we were experiencing". He attempted to whip up some controversy by bitching about the state of the English music industry and in particular the press and the year's most hyped band, Suede. "So, am I really supposed to be excited or even challenged by Suede?" he sniped. "I mean, I don't like to be cynical but if that really is the best that pop music can do in the space of a year or two, then there's no hope for the world.

"There's nothing that riles me about Suede. That's the whole point. It's not so much that they're manufactured, which they are, but that the product that's been manufactured isn't a particularly interesting one.

"There are adverts on the television that challenge me more than any song I've heard this year. There's more art in the Tango and Pot Noodle adverts than there is in Animal Nitrate or anything by Bikini Kill or Cornershop."

Radiohead's ugly duckling reputation in Britain remained intact through the summer as the band staggered from the stinging indifference of the media to outright scorn when the five-piece pulled out of the Reading Festival at the last minute.

"I woke up and I just couldn't speak, let alone sing," Yorke says of this low point. "I had people answering the phone for me.

"It was a combination of me feeling really run down and I just didn't want to do it. The pressure is fucking huge when you're in that situation and you have to ring up and say, 'Look, I can't do this' because that's not the end of it. You have to get a doctor's certificate, otherwise they'll sue you. I've been to see Harley Street specialists and they prescribed these steroid things for my voice that you inject into your neck. In the end I didn't take them. They're basically really nasty steroids. If you take them you won't be able to sing for a week but you will be able to get through tonight. I know Brett [from Suede] uses them a lot but I didn't."

When Radio One DJ Steve Wright read out an Evening Standard report about 'British Pop Unknowns Storm USA' during his afternoon show, he sealed their lowly status in the summer of '93. "I'm still upset that no one seems to care about us in Britain," whined Thom.

However, this situation changed when Creep came out again in the UK almost exactly a year after its first release. The single blasted into the Top 10 and was later voted Readers' Single of the Year in both Melody Maker and NME. It was only beaten by Take That's Pray as Radio One listeners' single of the year. Boosted by the success of the single, Pablo Honey eventually achieved Gold status in the UK.

Radiohead were in the States at the time of this re-issue, ploughing on into the American heartland and struggling to cope with the stress of the stamina-sapping schedule. Colin Greenwood's quick-witted, chatty personality alleviated some of the tension. Yorke: "Colin's great at talking to people when no one else will. He's our secret weapon. We wheel him out and he just doesn't shut up for half an hour. I can't even smile when all I want to do is punch someone in the face. Colin could smile while sticking a knife in your stomach. That's a huge compliment, by the way."

"For years it was a big problem that Colin and I never understood our moods. We never knew why we wigged out at each other, but when we did it was like a bomb going off. We're both very moody people. Now we're aware of that. we're very careful."

Colin and Ed O'Brien became regular room-mates on tour. "We choose partners – it's a personality thing," explains Colin. "Ed and I are both quite easy going, we're both smokers and we both have a soft spot for country soul music. You know, Dan Penn and Richard Buckner.

"I like sharing with Ed because he can do wicked Sean Connery and Darth Vader impressions first thing in the morning. He's crap for borrowing clothes off though, because he's so tall. I'd look like the incredible shrinking man in one of his jackets.

"The worst thing about Ed is his sleeptalking. One night he dreamt he was doing a radio show on Live 105 in San Francisco. He was going, 'Straight up after the break we've got another hot

> "Colin's great at talking to people when no one else will. He's our secret weapon. We wheel him out and he just doesn't shut up for half an hour.

I can't even smile when all I want to do is punch someone in the face. Colin could smile while sticking a knife in your stomach. That's a huge compliment, by the way."

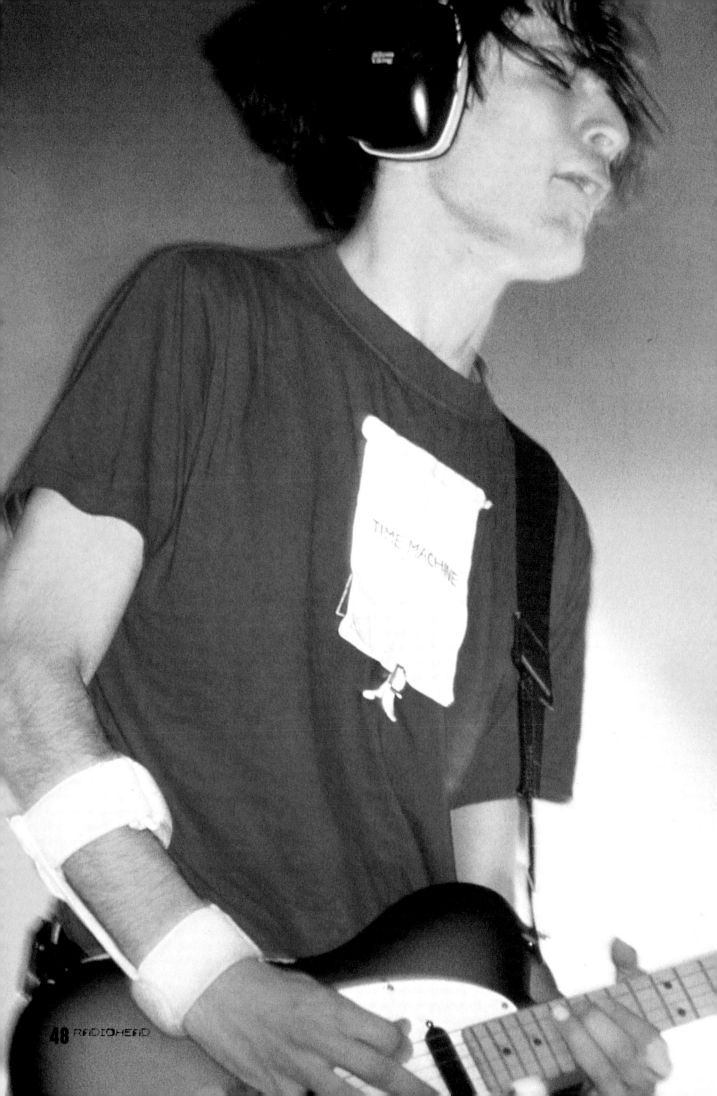

"I do wish I had my friends around to enjoy this sometimes," he admitted, "but even that's gone wrong because they've all gone to different universities as well and they're all graduating now. I think, I could be there doing that."

track from The Meters.' He even had a pause while he thought the record was playing, before introducing someone else. He kept that up for a good hour.

"We have this arrangement that if one of us brings a girl to the room, the other one disappears... I certainly couldn't pretend I was asleep and since Ed sounds like he's awake even when he's asleep, quite frankly it would be appalling."

However, during their 34-date autumn support slot for Belly, much of the good humour disappeared. Jonny Greenwood in particular became more introspective, shutting off the world by listening to BBC talking books on his Walkman. "I do wish I had my friends around to enjoy this sometimes," he admitted, "but even that's gone wrong because they've all gone to different universities as well and they're all graduating now. I think, I could be there doing that."

Colin remembers the band's support slot for Tears For Fears in Las Vegas in the Aladdin Theatre as their worst touring experience in America: "Normally Tom Jones would be playing there to 7,000 fans. We flew right across America to do this one gig, canceled a load of other things to do it, were told it was really, really important. Turned up and got told we'd be on at seven o'clock when there'd be nobody there. We got fucked over big-time by Tears For Fears. No soundcheck, moved about on the bill so we were opening, and we were assured we weren't going to be. And they were all complete wankers. But the joke was kind of on them because not only did Thom break all their lights during their set, but also for that night and for the rest of the tour they did a cover of Creep as their encore. Bizarre. He has to pay money for it, so that's cool. It was the ultimate irony."

Radiohead's mood was summed up by their intro music which was the doleful cello and piano of the Messiaen, scored in an old Silesian prison camp at the start of the century.

Darker still, in an NME interview Thom Yorke even confessed he actually considered leaving the band during the last few months of '93: "I thought I could go it alone. I thought I didn't need anybody, but I fucking do. It's so easy to think like that. It's such an easy frame of mind to lock yourself into and never get out of. As soon as you get any success you disappear up your own arse and you lose it for ever.

"When I got back to Oxford I was unbearable.

"I thought I could go it alone. I thought I didn't need anybody, but I fucking do. It's so easy to think like that. It's such an easy frame of mind to lock yourself into and never get out of. As soon as you get any success you disappear up your own arse and you lose it for ever.

You start to believe that you are this sensitive artist who has to be alone and you have to become this melodramatic, tortured person in order to create wonderful music. The absolute opposite is true, I think now. All those things happen to you anyway; you don't have to sit there and make them happen. Otherwise you're not a human being."

Characteristically for the slim-built, fragile singer, his mood swings went hand-in-hand with more illness. "We'd done a Belly tour, then a James tour – came off that and my back gave up. I got off a bus in San Francisco and couldn't move all day. Then when I got home in Oxford it was getting worse and worse... Even weirder things started happening. My joints had become hyper-mobile, so when I stopped working like that they just seized up. The joints were aching like I was an old man. It was fucking weird. It freaked me out so badly because just walking up the stairs was really painful."

This dramatic switch from pressurised activity to listless time-killing meant that he couldn't face his dark basement flat in Oxford. "I'm not someone who goes off for weeks on my own. I just let things go. I had a flat of my own for about six months and it's always a fucking tip. I'd always go home and go straight out again."

Fed up with the doomy atmosphere in his flat he bought a house. "I christened it The House That 'Creep' Built, 'cos I wouldn't have been able to buy it without the royalties. I didn't pay in cash though, 'cos I decided it might be the only money I ever make. I've got a nice little mortgage, 25 years, fixed rate, easy repayments. I didn't fancy the endowment mortgage. The guy took half an hour to explain it and I didn't understand it at all."

However, the mix of lethargy and edginess at the end of every tour meant that he continued to let things go to pot around him. "I bought this house and there were these two beautiful oriental fish that lived in a pond at the bottom of my garden," he says. "My other half went away for a few days and one of the things that was left on a note was 'look after the fish', because at the time there was snow and ice covering the ground. It was like two feet deep or something ridiculous. Now I let these fish die because I couldn't even be bothered to get my shit together to go down to the bottom of the garden and knock a little hole in the ice to keep these fish alive. So when I eventually remembered that they were there I saw them belly up in the ice, and one of them had his little mouth right next to the last hole that had been made there in the pond. A last gasp for breath."

Nevertheless there were some positive signals in the final months of 1993. Radiohead enjoyed supporting James in Europe, particularly at their massive G-Mex concert in December. More importantly, Yorke had managed to write "virtually half the [next] album in the back of the bus, with my tape recorder and guitar." 1994 offered the chance to get back into the studio and prove their worth.

Colin Greenwood:
"I think that within Radiohead's school of guitar noise there's a mid-tempo acoustic-ballads band struggling to get out. If we record enough albums and we're secure enough, perhaps we'll do a Neil Young Harvest album."

happen to you anyway; you don't have to sit there and make them happen. Otherwise you're not a human being."

"I could tell we'd held everything in because there wasn't enough energy there,"

THE BAND RETREATED to the Oxfordshire countryside in January 1994 to begin rehearsals for the next album. "The idea of coming to London to a big rehearsal studio is a nightmare to us because we all live in Oxford," says Jonny. "So we wanted a room that was completely ours, and also a room that wasn't like a rehearsal room. So basically we hired this old kind of shed on a fruit farm for five weeks, soundproofed it and put in a vocal PA and it was our space. It was great."

Fuelled by this bright start to the year, Radiohead went into RAK studios in St John's Wood on 28 February feeling confident about the new songs. This time they decided to get a new producer in, John Leckie, who is best known for his work with The Stone Roses. In fact, the band were more impressed by his production on Magazine's 1978 Real Life album, which was an old favourite of both Thom and the Greenwood brothers. Ed O'Brien was also enthusiastic about Leckie's involvement because the producer had worked with a Beatle in the early 70s: "John's great because he's from that old school of production where he was an apprentice at Abbey Road – his first session was assisting George Harrison and Phil Spector to record My Sweet Lord."

However, the recordings went wrong almost immediately as the tense, uncommunicative attitudes which stifled the band on their recent American tours suddenly resurfaced. "I could tell we'd held

says Yorke. "We were all crawling around the studio, not walking around."

We were really scared of our instruments

everything in because there wasn't enough energy there," says Yorke. "We were all crawling around the studio, not walking around. We were really scared of our instruments. That might sound over-dramatic but that's how it felt. It must have been tortuous to watch. I know it was very hard on our producer John Leckie who didn't know what the fuck was going on. We'd be going to him, 'So what do you think? What shall we do?' He was like, 'Well, I don't know, it's up to you. You can do what the fuck you like, just do it rather than sit there thinking about it.'"

The band refer to this period as their "worst" since forming in 1991, although Jonny's description of an "insidious and depressing" time is lightened by drummer Phil Selway's comical sense of English restraint. He sums up the band's implosion as "a time when in-band communication went to pot." Jonny is more forthcoming as he explains, "What happened was because of schedules – that dreaded word – it was suggested we record certain songs in a certain order so we'd have what people thought would be the singles recorded first. It was a very bad idea because it set the album on a really wrong track. The songs were sounding very good when we were rehearsing them but as soon as we'd work on a song for two weeks and then go back to one of the other songs, we'd forgotten it. So we ended up overrunning what was initially going to be two weeks and then we had to go on tour, and of course when we came back we ended up doing them all again."

According to John Leckie, the tracks earmarked as possible singles were The Bends, Sulk, Killer Cars and Nice Dream. "We did those and mixed them and the general opinion was that it was all a bit too manic," he detailed later. "The original version of The Bends was more overpowering than it is on record – it was a bit too much to take. The vocals were screaming more and things were cranked up more.

"Anyway, I went off to Abbey Road to mix those tracks and the band stayed in RAK to do some B-sides with the engineer and knocked out Black Star which of course ended up on the album.

"After the first three or four weeks of this period we all had a meeting and it was finally decided that they weren't going to release a single after all. So from there on in, there was an air of relief to the sessions. In the second month we did nearly all the tracks really, with overdubs and everything and then the band went off on tour in May.

"Nice Dream was one of the first things we recorded and it was quite simple really... There are some noises at the end of the solo part which we took from a tape I had of sounds of the Arctic which I got at Vancouver Aquarium. Just a daft idea of mine.

"Sulk was a bit of a problem for Thom because he wrote it when he was about sixteen about the Hungerford killings, and the last line was 'Just shoot your gun.' But he was worried about it as it didn't mean anything anymore and particularly after the Kurt thing, he didn't want to sing that. So he changed it to 'You'll never change.'"

Yorke remembers the "first breakthrough" came with the song Fake Plastic Trees. "That was one of the worst days for me. I spent the first five

The atmosphere within the band on tour was still fragile and highly charged as they travelled to the Far East, Australia, New Zealand and America in two summer spells which were originally booked to coincide with the release of their second album.

"You're either completely unable to talk to any kind of strangers or you're utterly overt and demand to meet them the next day," explains Thom. "I go between the two extremes. There's no middle ground."

or six hours at the studio just throwing a wobbly. I shouted at everyone and then John Leckie sent everybody away, 'but Thom stay here.' It was like being asked to stay after school. He sat me down and we did a guide vocal on Fake Plastic Trees. He set me up with a microphone and said, 'OK, play it' and that was the version we used."

When Radiohead left RAK they had a couple of promising demos and several recordings which, if released, would have set them up for ridicule as aspiring stadium pomp-rockers. "We had one song which had loads of strings and heavy guitars. It was all very epic and sounded like Guns N' Roses' November Rain," reveals Ed. By this time Yorke was "trying to shut off from everything. There was a lot of pressure for us to make a loud, bombastic record," he grimaces, "and all I ever wanted to do was the exact opposite."

The atmosphere within the band on tour was still fragile and highly charged as they travelled to the Far East, Australia, New Zealand and America in two summer spells which were originally booked to coincide with the release of their second album. "You're either completely unable to talk to any kind of strangers or you're utterly overt and demand to meet them the next day," explains

Thom. "I go between the two extremes. There's no middle ground."

Even the affable, even-tempered Ed O'Brien showed signs of cracking up.

Colin later recalled, "Ed has a reputation as the steady member of the band because he's usually so mellow. Last year ('94) in Los Angeles though, I think he was close to breaking. We were sitting in this nightmare restaurant with lousy service and lots of mobile phones going off and he just stood up and over-turned the entire table. He thought he was Jesus in The Temple Of Moneylenders."

However, the unhinged excitement of a Mexican tour in the summer proved to be a catalyst for a change in direction and attitude as most of the band start-ing to enjoy themselves again. Colin declares that "Guadalajara in Mexico" was one of the band's best gigs. "It was bonkers. We were four days into the Mexican tour, on the Mexican sleeping bus from hell. There were thirteen of us and six bunks. We arrived and everyone was pretty despondent. And the venue was this old theatre with no ceiling above the stage, one electrical socket and pigeon shit everywhere. And against all odds it was very cool. Phil hated it because there were five or six guys who refused to leave the stage, who claimed to be the guys who'd put up the lights. They just stood behind him, watching him drumming all night."

Another breakthrough was a show at London's Astoria on 27 May, which was taped for an MTV concert broadcast. "John Leckie came back after the show," recalls Yorke, "and he was like, 'Wow, you played all that note perfect. I can see now, I understand.'" Yorke later recorded his vocals over this live version of My Iron Lung, which all the band agreed couldn't be bettered in the studio.

Jonny Greenwood: "I strongly believe that

Ed has a reputation as the steady member of the band because he's usually so mellow. Last year ('94) in Los Angeles though, I think he was close to breaking. We were sitting in this nightmare restaurant with lousy service and lots of mobile phones going off and he just stood up and overturned the entire table. He thought he was Jesus in The Temple Of Moneylenders

Ed has a reputation as the steady member of the band because he's usually so mellow. Last year ('94) in Los Angeles though, I think he was close to breaking. We were sitting in this nightmare restaurant with lousy service and lots of mobile phones going off and he just stood up and overturned the entire table. He thought he was Jesus in The Temple Of Moneylenders

when a band play together for long enough something special is added. It sounds like there's something more going on than there is. That's what we did. That's why recording took so long because we wanted to get in the right frame of mind, and we did eventually."

The rejuvenated band went into The Manor studios in Oxfordshire for a two-week recording session from 16 to 30 June. "We finished nearly everything at our time there," says Leckie. "I think it helped that they'd been on tour because they had confidence in a lot of the songs again, which I think they'd maybe lost during that lengthy recording period. At one point, Thom was thinking about scrapping some of the songs and writing more."

On 1 August they relocated to Abbey Road for a month. Leckie: "During this time I mixed My Iron Lung and the six B-sides that went with it. It was an awful lot of work.

"When it came to mixing the album no one came! Then they started asking for copies of the multi-tracks and I realised they probably had someone else mixing the album as well and it turned out it was the same team who mixed the first album – the record company had been going on about trying to get an American sound for the record from the minute I got involved.

"The annoying thing for me a little bit was that there are things on there that they'd told me not to do originally – like using big reverbs on the voice or certain tones that were forbidden – that the Americans did. I found it quite funny. There's a lot to be said for other people mixing stuff because sometimes you get so into it that it's a good idea to have a fresh outlook on it with a total stranger. The finished product is a lot harder. I don't think I could have got it sounding quite as blasting as that."

The band took a bit of time off, enough for Phil to get married and go off on a honeymoon in

Lyme Regis. However, they faced a new disappointment when their return to the fray, the single My Iron Lung, was deemed "too heavy" for radio on its release in October '94. The fanbase took the song into the UK Top 30 where it stalled at 24. "People have defined our emotional range with that one song, Creep," complained Yorke, who was sick of the claustrophobic support system created by the success of that song. "I actually saw reviews of My Iron Lung which said it was just like 'Creep'. When you're up against things like that, it's like, 'fuck you'. These people are never going to listen."

My Iron Lung was a powerful, gutsy track, ranging from gorgeous, high-pitched vocals on the verse to an ugly chorus which echoed the visceral angst of Nirvana. Like Kurt Cobain's lyrics on Nirvana's 1993 In Utero album, Yorke was drawing on images stolen from medical journals to express himself. The title was inspired by a picture of an ill child inside an old 50s lung machine which the singer had come across at college. The contrast between the bulky mechanics and fragile body of the child, with just his head poking out of the top, influenced Yorke's college work and he used the picture for ideas for six months until he lost it.

The release of My Iron Lung also came with a further six new tracks including the Nick Drake-isms of Lozenge Of Love and You Never Wash Up where if you listen closely you can hear Phil set down his drum sticks halfway through and walk out. He thought it was just a rehearsal.

Meanwhile, over in the States, the lack of a successful follow-up to Creep had undermined the confidence of their US label Capitol, and they were actually getting cold feet about releasing a second album. "I mean, they hadn't heard it but we were just kind of discounting the Americans pretty much because they had us down as a pop act," said Jonny at the time. "Maybe releasing but certainly not pushing it, and making it their priority release for this year. We were feeling very low." But when the new sessions were finally delivered, "the bigwigs" at Capitol started ringing up enthusiastically and "telling us what to do, which was worse in a way," explained the young, long-limbed guitarist.

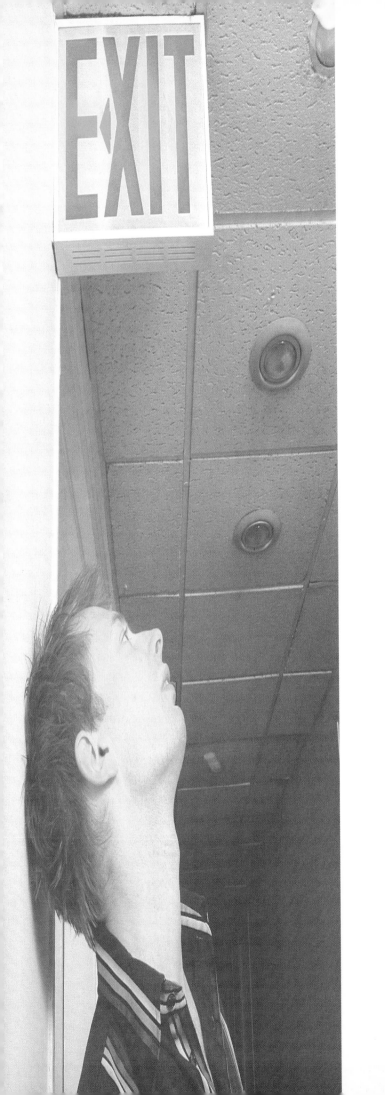

Thom Yorke:

"I think illness is creative; I haven't really been ill since we recorded The Bends. Nervous exhaustion was something I used to get an awful lot. I refused to do everything and used to end up doing most of it. Doing shows ten days in a row isn't very good for you. That was what used to make me snap."

"The Bends is completely jokey, completely taking the piss. None of that stuff had even happened to us when we wrote it. All that stuff about aeroplanes and not knowing who your real friends are, that was our Bowie pastiche. Our joke song!"

It kind of makes sense because we've all been on a cycle of illness. I've been run down with gastro-somethings, horrible things with Latin names that are attached to my lower intestines, which is great", he says perversely.

RELEASED IN MARCH '95, The Bends probed dark, emotionally traumatic themes with greater intensity than their debut album which often sacrificed real venom for rock posturing. Musically the album was taut and powerful, spewing out Yorke's lyrics with a fierce directness which was badly lacking in the good-time, Essex-boy cheeriness of Blur or the blinding, street romanticism of Suede. Although the album shared a greater affinity with Nirvana's In Utero, it wasn't a grunge record. By this time the American movement had lost its initial thrust, becoming a programmed, alternative style on American radio. Radiohead's music was far more charged and brutal in its self-hatred than the suspiciously self-conscious pain offered by the likes of Pearl Jam and Stone Temple Pilots. Certainly the stresses created by the massive success of Creep in the States fuelled some of this bitterness in Radiohead's songs. However, these experiences brought the band's own doubts and lack of confidence into focus, rather than transforming the whole record into a self-indulgent rant against fame. Yorke avoided songs about idealised relationships and rock 'n' roll fantasies, cutting right to the bone on the anatomical-sounding tracks like My Iron Lung, The Bends (a potentially fatal change of pressure in the blood which occurs when divers rise to the surface too quickly) and Bones. Jonny: "It's a real medical album for me. Thom went into a hospital to take pictures for the cover artwork, and it struck me the other day how much it's all about

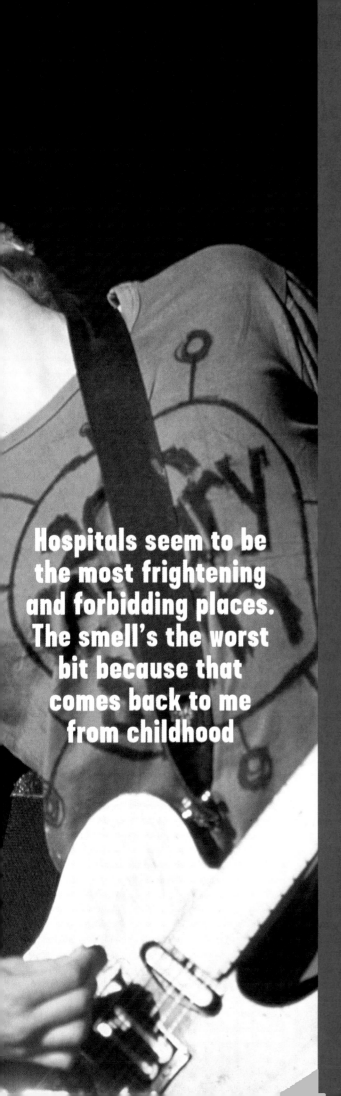

Hospitals seem to be the most frightening and forbidding places. The smell's the worst bit because that comes back to me from childhood

illness and doctors. It kind of makes sense because we've all been on a cycle of illness. I've been run down with gastro-somethings, horrible things with Latin names that are attached to my lower intestines, which is great", he says perversely. "There's also that feeling of revulsion about your own body," he adds. "That resentment that you're so reliant on it. Just looking at your hands all the time and seeing all the bones. Urgh.

"I think it's a fairly new way of describing relationships. All Thom's stuff is about drip-feeds and life-support systems. Even the cover is from a hospital. Thom went in and filmed those inflatable dummies that you breathe into."

Yorke: "I'm completely fascinated with that kind of imagery, the technological human imagery. Hospitals seem to be the most frightening and forbidding places. The smell's the worst bit because that comes back to me from childhood.

"A lot of this record is about me trying to shut off from everything and create my own little dreamy environment, in which to exist rather than have to deal with all the shit. I mean it wasn't really a dramatic amount of shit, it was my way of dealing with it. I'm not saying, Oh I'm such a tortured artist; it was a reaction to what was around me.

"The Bends is cynical and nervous and not making sense. You get the feeling at the end of it that there's something wrong, but you can't work out what it is."

When I met Thom in Oxford he ran through the album track by track:

Planet Telex

"I was off my head when I did it. It was four o'clock in the morning and John Leckie said, 'We've got to do the vocal now.' Ed remembers it more, but apparently I sang it all with my head on the floor because I couldn't stand up. I was bent double and I hadn't a clue what I was singing.

"We nicked Planet Telex from Tago Mago by Can. We're arty, us."

The Bends

"We wrote this song before we finished the first album. The sound at the beginning comes from this caterwauling mayhem outside this hotel in the States. There was this guy training these eight-year-old kids, who were parading up and down with all these different instruments. The guy had this little microphone on his sweater and was going: "Yeah, keep it up, keep it up.' So I ran out and taped it."

High And Dry

"It's a demo we did two years ago. We'd all completely forgotten about it and then someone dug it up and said: 'Hey, listen to this.' We had to go into the rehearsal and completely re-learn it. It has this real naive charm that offsets everything else."

Fake Plastic Trees

"I had a week in Los Angeles which is the longest time I've spent there – one of the things I discovered was that most of the women in Hollywood are desperate to find the perfect man, and most of the men are desperate to shag around and bugger off. Then occasionally you catch glimpses of these really lonely people, especially the women. The men are just screwing around and it was really sad.

   "Last night I was called by the American record company insisting, well almost insisting, that we used a Bob Clearmountain mix of it. I said: 'No way.' All the ghost-like keyboard sounds and weird strings were completely gutted out of his mix, like he'd gone in with a razor blade and chopped it all up. It was horrible."

Bones

"We recorded this about four times before we got it right. The original had the ending going on for about a minute and a half, which was something Jonny got from The Fall."

Nice Dream

"We all debuted playing acoustic guitar on that in a sort of cosmic Kumbaya outside in the studio. There's this awful photograph of us all sitting on a lawn with headphones on. The lyrics came out of a half-drunk dream I had, one of those where you don't really sleep properly. It's about our relationship with people generally."

Just (Do It To Yourself)

"I love the really high notes at the end, which don't even sound like a guitar. I went away from the studio for a day and Jonny worked on it. When I came back and heard what he'd done, I thought it was the most exciting thing I've ever heard us come up with on tape."

My Iron Lung

"It was written during the James/Belly tour in 1993 when we'd really had enough and didn't want to go on any more. We were being plugged in every day like a jukebox."

Bulletproof

"It's probably my favourite, but we thought it was a bit slow and timid at first. Then we taped the guitarists without them knowing where they were on the track and they came up with these weird noises at just the right moments. It was completely indulgent but it sounded great, like a lot of trains going past."

Black Star

"My favourite thing about this song is Jonny's guitar when it comes in on the chorus. It was completely crazy afterwards because everyone was saying: 'We've got to do the guitar again because it sounds such a mess.' Me and Jonny were going: 'No, no, no.'"

Street Spirit

"It was written around the time of My Iron Lung and was one of those songs that completely wrote itself. It was all coming out of this one riff. I love stuff like Stereolab where they repeat riffs over and over again."

Sulk

"This was the last one we did. There's thousands of tambourines on it, but you can't really hear it on the final mix. It was a weird song because it went from being the one that the record company insisted was going to be the hit to the least-liked thing on the album."

Jonny on Thom:

"Thom's unbelievably productive and creative. He would happily spend the rest of his life writing and recording songs instead of performing."

RADIOHEAD 7

At the same time, nervous about the album's reception, the singer tore into the "incestuous" nature of the British music industry with all the zeal and bitterness of a discredited heretic. "Other bands really wind me up. I'm very competitive and antagonistic. I just hate meeting other bands. I read this quote from Portishead about the NME's Brat Awards and the guy said, 'I don't know what I'm doing here really, it's just a lot of indie bands drinking loads of beer and shouting at each other across the tables.' That's why I don't like it. The British music scene is so insular, so petty and so fucking bitchy I just don't want to have any contact with it. That's why we've never moved to London. If we did, that would be it. We'd last a month and then split up." He summed up his two-fingered stance by stating, "It doesn't bother me that we're not accepted in England. I'm rather hoping that we stay like this for a few years. I think we've got the biggest fan base in Britain and ultimately I don't really give a fuck. In a bloody-minded way I hope we're left alone. I thrive on being an outsider. I think the worst thing that could happen is if a British music paper put us on the cover saying that we're the best band in Britain. Although," he added with a smile, "it's not very likely that will happen."

Instead he psyched himself up for another face-off with Radiohead's critics. "I don't want this record to sound that self-indulgent and self-referential because I don't think it is. If the music doesn't go beyond our own experiences then the whole point of making this record is lost", he snarled with a touch of melodrama. "The one thing I can see people slagging us off for is that, but that's because they're not listening to the music."

He needn't have worried. David Sinclair of The Times described The Bends as "the album of the decade". Others summed Radiohead up as "the U2 it's OK to like" or even more flatteringly, "the next REM."

Many critics focused on the bitter, self-absorbed moods of the album. NME described "a none-too-subtle sense of fragility, a feeling of physical fatalism". The Guardian ruminated at length on the personality of Thom Yorke: "He is predictably, a mass of contradictions: a strange blend of snide cynicism, bitter self-pity and earnest decency. There is still something studenty about him – his juvenile sense of humour, his naff sense of outsiderness; his naively radical idealism."

The New York Times was more dramatic in its appraisal of Yorke's state of mind: "The world is caving in on Thom Yorke. He has no real friends."

The singer's attempt to deflect from his own personality through more oblique lyrics than those on Pablo Honey had clearly failed. The songs were not as openly personal as the autobiographical bloodletting of Sinead O'Connor or Hole but Jonny hints at the truth when he says, "All Thom's songs eventually come down to how he's feeling." The mustard-haired frontman insists that "I don't think we always write about fraught anxieties... well, I'm trying not to."

Their reputation for angst-ridden melancholy spread as far as Hollywood when a character in the movie Clueless summed up Radiohead as "cry-baby music." "Cool!" responds Thom. "I mean, I suppose it does piss me off but I am a moaning cry-baby from hell, really. Besides, the characters in that film aren't the kind of people I'd want to like Radiohead. They're just average, two-dimensional Beverly Hills kids, and the person who is actually listening to us in the film is the only three-dimensional character. So the answer is: 'Fuck you, we're for 3D people!'

"Some famous pop star told me to lighten up. And I felt really proud of myself. I felt really good because I haven't lightened up. I have absolutely no intention of lightening up because when I do I

The New York Times was more dramatic in its appraisal of Yorke's state of mind: "The world is caving in on Thom Yorke.

really will turn into Jim Kerr".

However, back in '95 he also insisted he wasn't going to become a self-destructive martyr: "There's this pernicious feeling creeping into things that because everything is second-hand, and we're all so post-modern, that the only way to transcend this is to throw yourself to the lions, cut yourself up, or go on heroin. In order to mean it. I no longer feel that I have to prove that I mean it."

The Bends has sold 1.5 million copies world-wide since its release, achieving platinum status in the UK (300,000 sales) and Canada (100,000), while in the States it has so far totalled 800,000. After all the fuss about finding a single at the start of 1994, the first single from the album was an old demo version of High And Dry. John Leckie tells the story: "I said to the record company that I thought it was amazing and it was the best one, but the view from the band was that it was too good for this record and they were going to save it for the next one. So it was put aside and never mentioned. We finished everything else, mixed it all and then High And Dry came up, and we hadn't heard it for a year, so we put on the tape and decided to go with it. The one on the album is the demo version. It's strange as well that after all the worry about singles, this is the one that eventually went out just before the album."

In the band's new promo video for the single High And Dry, Thom tried to re-claim the Creep monster for himself by wearing one of the American promotional badges which declares, 'I am a creep'.

High And Dry's solid but unspectacular sales in the British Top 20 set the tone for the follow-up singles. Fake Plastic Trees and Just (Do It To Yourself) (which was accompanied by an intriguing sub-titled video featuring a man who is lying on the ground for a reason only discernible through lip-reading at the end) also failed to breach the Top 10 in the UK. Furthermore unlike their Britpop rivals Pulp, Blur, Oasis, Suede and Supergrass in 1995 and 1996, Radiohead failed to win either a Brit Award or the Mercury Music Prize. Although they gained critical and commercial recognition in the UK after the release of The Bends, they were still 'outsiders' who existed apart from the hyped-up, jingoistic euphoria surrounding Britpop.

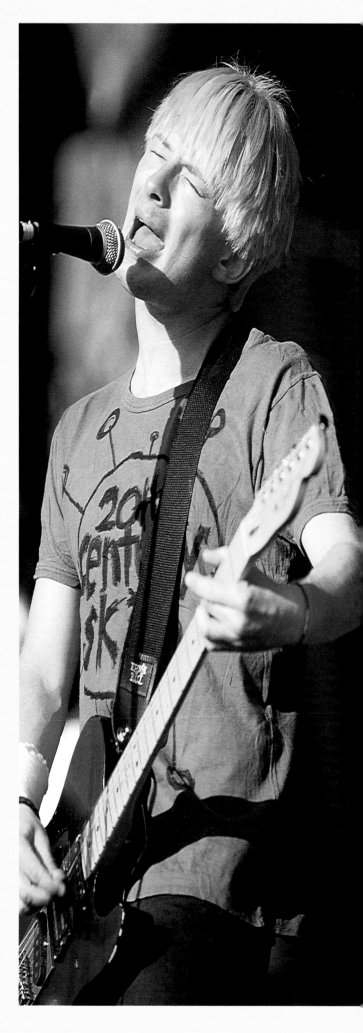

There's this pernicious feeling creeping into things that because everything is second-hand, and we're all so post-modern, that the only way to transcend this is to throw yourself to the lions, cut yourself up, or go on heroin. In order to mean it. I no longer feel that I have to prove that I mean it

onny on Thom:
Apart *from the band, Thom's only
bsession is clothes. If he has a
ay off he'll spend it shopping.
'e's wearing a lot of my tops these
ays. They look better on him than
ne and it stops him wearing those
ght, long-sleeved women's shirts
e used to be into."*

RADIOHEAD PROMOTED The Bends for the rest of 1995, including a prestigious support slot from July to October on REM's world tour. Both bands enjoyed the experience. Michael Stipe conceded, "I'm frightened by how good they are" while Thom Yorke gushed in a diary written for Q magazine: "Shit, shit, shit. This is REM and they really like us. No, I mean they really like us."

Colin: "It's been brilliant. I mean, I remember listening to Reckoning and things on my Walkman on my way to exams at school, you know? And they've been so good to us, and it's been really, really good for us. Especially Thom. This seems to have been his year for meeting his heroes. Like, Elvis Costello came up and introduced himself at this thing we did in Italy. I think that kind of thing has helped him a lot."

In August, three days before they set off on the American leg of the REM tour, Radiohead recorded a new track, Lucky, for War Child's Help album which raised money for children in Bosnia. Ed O'Brien: "The whole idea of doing a record for Bosnia is great, but I think that John Lennon thing of doing a record in one day captured a lot of people's imaginations. It speaks for itself that so many bands are doing it.

"It's very easy for us to be cynical about music, but I think it is one of those things that unites people."

Melody Maker was so impressed by Lucky they declared "Radiohead are no longer capable of anything other than brilliance."

For many people who bought the album, this bitter-sweet ballad was the standout track, but when it was released as a War Child single later in the year Radio One once again backed off and failed to give it daytime airplay.

As The Bends tour continued in the autumn, Yorke recalled a typically off-beat incident as a personal highlight. "There was an incident in Finland, where we did this arts festival. We'd done one encore, and came on for another one, and I noticed this girl down the front going, 'Get off, get off' to some bloke. And he was basically feeling her up, this bloke, behind her, and this girl was really frantic. But he was also the guy who'd jumped on to stage three or four

"The whole idea of doing a record for Bosnia is great, but I think that John Lennon thing of doing a record in one day captured a lot of people's imaginations. It speaks for itself that so many bands are doing it"

songs beforehand.

"So the best moment of the show for me was when after having molested this girl and me gone over and made faces at him, he climbed on to the stage again and received my guitar in his bollocks. Such a graceful movement. Made my day."

Although exhilarated by his experiences, Yorke was still suffering from bouts of illness. In October 1995 he complained, "I've got fluid in my ears and it makes me hypersensitive. I'm going to have to wear earplugs, I think, for the soundcheck and the show." He insisted on seeing "one doctor in each city if necessary", and worried that these were early signs of deafness which runs in his family. There was another dark incident in Germany, described by the NME as "Thom's tantrum". "I freaked out," he allows. "I couldn't sing. Threw stuff around. The amp, the drum kit...I had blood all over my face. I cried for two hours afterwards." He was ill, couldn't deal with the strange medication and his voice was cracking up.

On a more positive note, in addition to Lucky, Radiohead started playing some new material - a rough version of a new song Subterranean Homesick Alien, described by Yorke as "like the Dylan song, but not" and another called No Surprises Please. Thom also welcomed kisses from his fans, undermining his surly, hands-off reputation: "It's nice. It's the only kiss I get. It's the only time I get any physical contact with anybody."

In 1996 Street Spirit (Fade Out) was released as a single, backed by four new songs: Bishop's Robes, Talk Show Host, Banana Co. and Molasses. After a long period of muted chart success in the singles chart, Street Spirit broke into the Top 10 at number five, partly thanks to the interest generated by the accompanying video. Directed by Jonathon Glazer, the promo made use of a special camera which is capable of tracking the progress of a bullet from a gun. Yorke: "In this video we wanted to make something really elegant and beautiful. The song came out of a stream of consciousness and Jonathon Glazer and I wanted something that would create space in the viewer's imagination to complement this. Pop videos so often kill a

song stone dead, but when Jonathon suggested using the photosonics ultra-slow motion science camera coupled with reference to the surrealist photographers of the early century, we knew we had something."

The rest of the year was spent rehearsing and recording new songs in Oxfordshire. They aired three unreleased tracks at the T In The Park Festival, Strathcylde, in July – Electioneering, which was summed up as "pretty upbeat – an almost Clash-style skiffle" by the Guardian; Airbag, outlined by the newspaper as "another scrape with Yorke's mortal self" and the afore-mentioned No Surprises Please.

Since disappearing back to these studio sessions, they've also recorded a song called Lift, featuring Jonny on keyboards, and I Promise, which Yorke has spoken of as "about faith, in, er, a relationship. It's supposed to be quite positive." In 1997 the singer appears to be ready to trash his dour, fragile media image in order to create the most forward-looking music of Radiohead's career to date: "All of us have been given great belief in ourselves. It's like a flash of release more than inspiration. I know we can do it now. The next album will be about that release. The way we're writing and the way we feel when we play together is about release now. And the new stuff is grateful and will hopefully be good because of that. I have every intention that the next album will be a very grateful record.

"I love life. I really do. But there's so much shit to deal with. Like I have friends who are artists. Good artists. Maybe even great artists. But they're at the end of their tethers. What with the dole, the poverty, they just don't have the energy to carry on. When we started this thing, I really did believe, 'The good will out. The best rises to the top.' But I no longer believe that. People are continuously overlooked and ignored... It's not just artists. It's everybody.

"If I was happy, I'd be in a fucking car advert. A lot of people think they're happy, and they live these boring lives and do the same things every day. But one day they wake up and realise they haven't lived yet. I'd much rather celebrate the highs and lows of everyday life than try to deny them."

I love life. I really do. But there's so much shit to deal with. Like I have friends who are artists. Good artists. Maybe even great artists. But they're at the end of their tethers. What with the dole, the poverty, they just don't have the energy to carry on. When we started this thing, I really did believe, 'The good will out. The best rises to the top.

"If I was happy, I'd be in a fucking car advert. A lot of people think they're happy, and they live these boring lives and do the same things every day. But one day they wake up and realise they haven't lived yet. I'd much rather celebrate the highs and lows of everyday life than try to deny them."

DISCOGRAPHY:

Albums:
March 93
PABLO HONEY (25)
You Creep/How Do You?/Stop Whispering/Thinking About You/Anyone Can Play The Guitar/Ripcord/Vegetable/Prove Yourself/ I Can't/Lurgee/Blowout

March 95
THE BENDS (6)
Planet Telex/The Bends/High and Dry/Fake Plastic Trees/Bones/Nice Dreams/Just (Do it yourself)/ My Iron Lung/Bullet Proof/Black Star/Sulk/Spirit.

Singles:

September 92
DRILL EP
Prove Yourself/Stupid Car/Thinking about you)

December 92
Creep/Lurgee/Inside my Head/Million Dollar Question

February 93
Anyone Can Play Guitar/Faithless/The Wonder Boy/Coke Babies(32)

May 93
Pop is Dead/Banana Co/Creep (live)/Ripcord (live)(42)

October 94
My Iron Lung/The Trickster/Lewis (Mistreated)/Punch Drunk Lovesick Singalong/Lozenge of Love/Permanent Daylight/You

Never Washup After Yourself(24)

March 94
High and Dry/Planet Telex/Maquii Adora/Killer Cars (17)

May 95
Fake Plastic Trees/India Rubber/How Can You Be Sure?/Bulletproof (20)

August 95
Just (Do it for Yourself)/Planet Telex/Bones (Live) Anyone Can Play Guitar (Live) (19)

October 95
Help EP

January 96
Street Spirit (Fade Out)/Banana Co/Molasses (5)

SOURCES

CHAPTER ONE
VOX
Steve Malins
SELECT
Gina Morris
NME
Ted Kessler
ROLLING STONE
Jon Wiederhorn
MELODY MAKER
The Stud Brothers
MELODY MAKER
Caitlin Moran
VOX
Mark Sutherland
MAKING MUSIC
Tom Doyle
MELODY MAKER
Paul Lester
MELODY MAKER
Dave Jennings
MELODY MAKER
Band File
RECORD COLLECTOR
Pat Gilbert

CHAPTER TWO
NME
Ted Kessler
VOX
Steve Malins
VOX
Mark Sutherland
MAKING MUSIC
Tom Doyle
VARSITY CAMBRIDGE
Ed Halliwell
CURFEW
Ronan
DAZED & CONFUSED
Lisa Verrico
ROLLING STONE
Jon Wiederhorn
RECORD COLLECTOR
Pat Gilbert
MELODY MAKER
Paul Lester
SELECT
Gina Morris
MELODY MAKER
The Stud Brothers
NME
Simon Williams

CHAPTER THREE
DAZED & CONFUSED
Lisa Verrico
MELODY MAKER
Band File
CURFEW
Ronan
VOX
Steve Malins
SELECT
Gina Morris
ROLLING STONE
Glenn Kenny
MELODY MAKER
Paul Lester
MELODY MAKER
Peter Paphides
MELODY MAKER
Dave Jennings
EVENING STANDARD
Tim Cooper
OBSERVER LIFE
Roger Tedre
NME
Ted Kessler
MELODY MAKER
Andrew Mueller
NME
Simon Williams
VOLUME
Craig McLean

CHAPTER FOUR
DAZED & CONFUSED
Lisa Verrico
ROLLING STONE
Jon Wiederhorn
VOX
Steve Malins
VOLUME
Craig McLean
NME
Stuart Ballie
DAZED & CONFUSED
Jefferson Heck/Thom Yorke
MELODY MAKER
Andrew Mueller
MELODY MAKER
The Stud Brothers
SELECT
Gina Morris
THE GUARDIAN
Jim Shelley
MELODY MAKER
Holly Barringer
MELODY MAKER
Dave Jennings
MUSIC & MEDIA
Machigiel Bakker
MELODY MAKER
Peter Paphides
VOX
Mark Sutherland

CHAPTER FIVE
VOLUME
Craig McLean
VOX
Steve Malins
ROLLING STONE
(New Faces: Presented by Chevrolet)
MELODY MAKER
Holly Barringer
MELODY MAKER
Jennifer Nine
MELODY MAKER
Tom Doyle
MAKING MUSIC
Tom Doyle
NME
Stuart Bailie

CHAPTER SIX
VOX
Steve Malins
THE TIMES
David Sinclair
THE GUARDIAN
Jim Shelley
THE NEW YORK TIMES
review of The Bends: as quoted in The Guardian
MELODY MAKER
Caitlin Moran
NME
Andy Richardson
TIME OUT
Peter Paphides
NME
Simon Willaims
MELODY MAKER
Tom Doyle
VOX
Mark Sutherland
MELODY MAKER
Andrew Mueller
SMASH HITS
Helen Lamont
DAZED & CONFUSED
Jefferson Heck/Thom Yorke
THE OBSERVER

CHAPTER SEVEN
VOX
Steve Malins
DAZED & CONFUSED
Lisa Verrico
Q MAGAZINE
Thom Yorke's Diary
MELODY MAKER
Andrew Mueller
NME
Simon Williams
THE GUARDIAN
Jim Shelley
ROLLING STONE
Jon Wiederhorn
THE TIMES
Caitlin Moran
SUNDAY MAIL
Russell Blackstock
THE INDEPENDENT
Ryan Gibley
MELODY MAKER
The Stud Brothers
MELODY MAKER
news story
VOX
Mark Sutherland
NME news story
ALTERNATIVE PRESS
RAW

PICTURES

RETNA:
Front cover and pages 1, 4-5, 8, 9, 10, 11, 18, 21, 24, 27, 28-29, 30, 31, 32, 34-35, 37, 40, 43, 44-45, 52, 76, 82-83.

ALL ACTION:
2-3, 6-7, 12, 13, 14-15, 16, 23, 33, 48-49, 51, 64-65, 74-75, 78, 80.

PAT POPE:
55, 56, 60, 61, 86, 88-89, 90.